THE HISTORY OF SPACE EXPLORATION

DAWN OF THE SPACE AGE

ROBIN KERROD

WORLD ALMANAC® LIBRARY

Please visit our web site at:
www.worldalmanaclibrary.com
For a free color catalog describing
World Almanac® Library's list of high-quality
books and multimedia programs, call
1-800-848-2928 (USA) or **1-800-387-3178
(Canada).** World Almanac® Library's fax:
(414) 332-3567.

Library of Congress Cataloging-in-Publication Data

Kerrod, Robin.
    Dawn of the space age / by Robin Kerrod.
       p. cm. — (The history of space exploration)
    Includes bibliographical references and index.
    ISBN 0-8368-5705-4 (lib. bdg.)
    ISBN 0-8368-5712-7 (softcover)
    1. Astronautics—History—Juvenile literature.
I. Title. II. Series.
TL793.H457   2004
629.4'09—dc22   2004041944

First published in 2005 by
World Almanac® Library
330 West Olive Street, Suite 100
Milwaukee, WI 53212 USA

Copyright © 2005 by World Almanac® Library.

Developed by White-Thomson Publishing Ltd
Editor: Veronica Ross
Designer: Gary Frost, Leishman Design
Picture researcher: Elaine Fuoco-Lang

World Almanac® Library editor: Carol Ryback
World Almanac® Library designer: Kami Koenig
World Almanac® Library art direction: Tammy West

Photo credits: top (t), bottom (b), left (l), right (r)
All images used with the permission of NASA except:
Bettmann/CORBIS 20; Jonathan Blair/CORBIS 18; Gu
Motil/CORBIS 6; Institute of Civil Engineers/Mary Eva
8(t); Popperfoto 14, 17(t), 17(b); Space Charts Photo
Library 5, 22(b), 24, 28, 29, 30(b), 34, 36, 37(t) 37(b
38, 40, 41, 42, 43(b). Artwork by Peter Bull.

Printed in Canada

1 2 3 4 5 6 7 8 9 09 08 07 06 05 04

Cover image: A Little Joe rocket blasting into space.

*Title page: A Saturn 1 launch vehicle at the Kennedy Spa
Center's Visitor Center.*

*Contents page: An Applications Technology Satellite bein
tested at the Johnson Space Center in the 1970s.*

▼ *The X-15 space plane hangs beneath the right wing of
an enormous B-52 "superfortress" bomber. The X-15
launched from the larger plane at an altitude of about
45,000 feet (14,000 meters).*

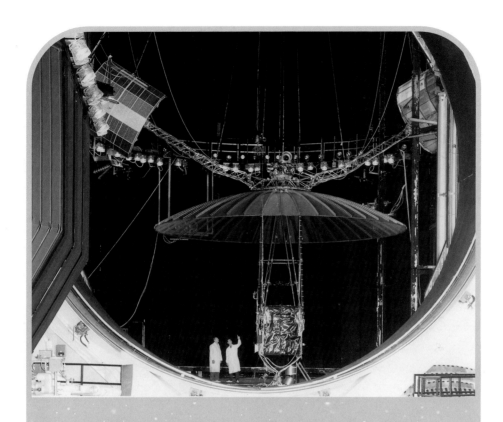

CONTENTS

FROM DREAMS TO REALITY

All the heavenly bodies we see in the night sky—the Moon, the planets, the stars, and the galaxies—travel through space. Altogether, planets, moons, stars, and galaxies, and space itself, make up the Universe.

One of the most dominant forces in the Universe is the force of gravity, the attraction, or pull, of one body on another. Earth's spin and its mass helps create the gravity that holds us and everything else down on the ground. The Sun's gravity keeps Earth and the other planets circling in their orbits. The gravity of the stars keeps them together in great star islands, or galaxies, and the gravity of the galaxies holds them together to form our gigantic Universe.

People began exploring space in their imagination a long time before they developed the means to travel there. Many authors described ingenious methods of traveling to the Moon. About 1658, celebrated French novelist and swordsman Cyrano de Bergerac argued that he could overcome the force of gravity and fly into space by attaching bottles of dew to his body. When the early morning Sun evaporated the dew into the air, he would go up with it.

The heroes in *From the Earth to the Moon* (1865), by the French novelist Jules Verne, sped to the Moon in a hollow shell fired from a giant cannon. Coincidentally, their launch site was in Florida, not far from where the first real Moon missions launched a century later.

In England, H. G. Wells wrote about Martians invading Earth in *The War of the Worlds* (1898). His chosen method of transporting people to the Moon in *The First Men in the Moon* (1901) used an antigravity material called cavorite. Exposing the cavorite to Earth cut off Earth's gravity, allowing the Moon's gravity to pull spacecraft toward it.

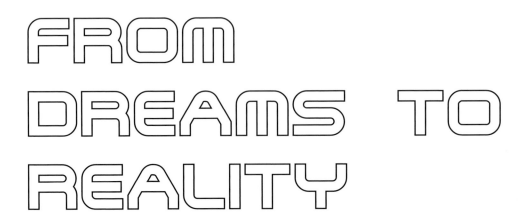

▶ *A view of deep space from the Hubble Space Telescope. A few galaxies are scattered here and there, but mostly space is empty.*

CHAPTER ONE

ROCKETING INTO SPACE

Early science-fiction writers such as Verne and Wells overlooked a suitable device for launching people into space—the rocket. Its basic style actually changed very little since its invention by the Chinese in the thirteenth century A.D.

▲ *Space rockets and fireworks work on the same principle as the very first Chinese rockets developed centuries ago.*

When you throw a ball, it travels a certain distance until gravity makes it drop to the ground. Throw the ball harder, and it travels faster and farther before gravity once again pulls it down to the ground. Speed helps the ball overcome gravity for a few seconds. This same principle allows us to use speed to launch objects into space.

The path a satellite takes around Earth is called its orbit. The speed at which a satellite travels is called its orbital velocity. To put an object into Earth orbit, we must boost it to an average minimum altitude of 90 miles (144 kilometers) at a speed of 17,500 miles per hour (28,000 kilometers per hour) in a direction parallel with the ground. At this speed the object remains in space circling Earth. Gravity still tugs at it, but as the speeding object falls toward the ground, the Earth's surface curves away beneath it at an equal rate: The object stays in space and becomes a satellite of Earth.

BY REACTION

Isaac Newton's third law of motion states that for every action (force in one direction), there is an equal and opposite reaction (force in the opposite direction). A rocket's burning fuel produces hot gases that escape from a nozzle at high speed. The force of the gases shooting out the opposite end of the rocket

CHINESE ARROWS OF FIRE

The first known use of rockets occurred in 1232, when the Chinese used "arrows of flying fire" in their war against the Mongols. These burning missiles probably consisted of arrows with tubes of gunpowder attached. The Chinese invented gunpowder at some point before 1000 A.D. Over the centuries, they developed rockets into more effective missiles by fitting them with gunpowder charges designed to explode or set things on fire. By the 1800s, improvements by Englishman William Congreve and others created more accurate and destructive rocket weapons, and most armies boasted a rocket squadron.

▼ An early Chinese rocketeer prepares to launch a rocket.

creates an equal and opposite force that propels it forward. Rockets work in space because they carry their own supply of oxygen to burn the fuel. (No ordinary engine is powerful enough to boost an object into orbital velocity, which is more than ten times the speed of a rifle bullet, and no ordinary engine works in space.) A normal engine uses oxygen in the air to help burn its fuel. But there is no air in space.

Rocket fuel consists of solid or liquid substances, called propellants, that propel it into space. The propellants must contain fuel and an oxidizer, a substance that provides oxygen. Gunpowder, which burns easily in the atmosphere, served as the propellant for the early, earthbound rockets.

Rocket fuel can be either solid or liquid. Some modern space rockets use solid propellants, but most use the more powerful liquid propellants. Kerosene and liquid oxygen are two widely used liquid propellants—mostly used in the rockets that launched Soviet (now Russian) spacecraft. The U.S. space shuttles' main engines use two other liquid propellants—hydrogen and liquid oxygen.

THE FATHER OF ASTRONAUTICS

A deaf Russian school teacher named Konstantin Tsiolkovsky (1857–1935) proposed the use of liquid hydrogen and oxygen for use as rocket propellant more than a century ago in 1903. That year, he also published *Exploring Space with Reactive Devices*. ("Reactive devices" means "rockets.") The book

▲ Konstantin Tsiolkovsky, who lived in Kaluga, Russia, near Moscow, from 1892 until his death in 1935. His house is now a museum.

detailed his experiments on rocket flight and the prospects of space travel.

Tsiolkovsky developed his intense interest in rocketry in his early teens. Russia had a formidable rocket squadron in those days. By the time he reached age twenty-one, Tsiolkovsky was convinced that rockets could be used for space travel.

In 1883, Tsiolkovsky, who was now a school teacher, wrote the book *Free Space*, in which he imagined flying around Earth in a spaceship.

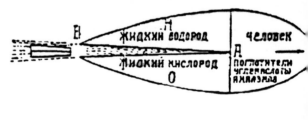

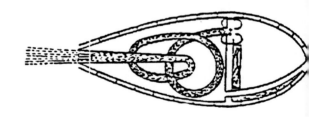

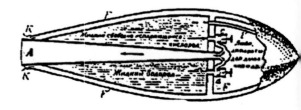

▶ *Three illustrations of rockets drawn by Tsiolkovsky. The top drawing (1903), which shows a rocket powered by liquid hydrogen and liquid oxygen propellants, is the earliest drawing of a liquid-propellant rocket. The middle drawing (1911) shows hot gases circulating in two rings at right angles to each other. It illustrates the idea that the forces of gases moving in different directions would help steady the rocket. The bottom illustration (1915) shows a liquid hydrogen/liquid oxygen rocket with valves to control propellant flow.*

◀ *This print from 1821 shows a rocket squadron launching rockets to repel a cavalry charge (upper image) and to storm a town (lower image). These rocket weapons shot iron balls at the enemy to inflict injury or carried incendiary charges to cause fires.*

"Mankind will not remain forever on the Earth. In pursuit of light and space he will timidly at first probe the limits of the atmosphere and later extend his control throughout the solar system."
Konstantin Tsiolkovsky in 1911.

He predicted the effects of weightlessness. In another book, *A Dream of Earth and Sky* (1895), he mentioned the possibility of artificial Earth satellites. In all, Tsiolkovsky put forward so many ideas about space travel that he is often called the father of astronautics—the science of traveling in space.

PIONEERING AERONAUTICS

Tsiolkovsky thought seriously about rocket space travel long before anyone ever flew through the air in an airplane. By coincidence, however, he published his *Reactive Devices* book the same year as the first airplane flight: 1903. That year, on December 17, in Kitty Hawk, North Carolina, brothers Orville and Wilbur Wright from Dayton, Ohio, took turns at the controls of their gasoline-powered biplane. Orville made the first flight, traveling just 120 feet (37 meters) in twelve seconds. The brothers logged three more flights that same day. On the fourth flight, Wilbur flew the plane for 852 feet (260 m), staying airborne for fifty-nine seconds. Although the plane's flights were brief, they demonstrated the possibility of engine-powered, heavier-than-air flight. The event signaled the beginning of the development of modern air travel and helped lead to space travel.

▼ *On December 17, 1903, Orville Wright piloted the world's first flying machine as his brother, Wilbur, watched. This historic flight marked the beginning of aviation as we know it today.*

Ironically, Tsiolkovsky was essentially a thinker rather than a doer. He never built any rockets himself.

"MOONY" GODDARD

The practical beginnings of space rocketry in fact occurred half a world away from Tsiolkovsky, in Worcester, Massachusetts, where Robert Hutchings Goddard was born in 1882. Goddard became fascinated with rockets and space travel after reading the stories of Jules Verne and H. G. Wells.

In 1911, Goddard received a doctorate from Clark University in Worcester and became professor of physics there. He made many improvements in rocket design and gained 214 patents for them. During World War I (1914–1918), Goddard move to California to work on rocket devices for the military, returning to Clark University afterward.

In 1919, Goddard wrote a paper entitled "A Method of Reaching Extreme Altitudes," which outlined the current state of rocketry and its possib future. Among other things, he suggested launchin a rocket to impact the New Moon. Upon impact, it would ignite a powerful flash, which astronomers could see through their telescopes. This idea was so

▲ Robert Goddard teaching physics at Clark University, Worcester, Massachusetts, in 1924. The blackboard diagram shows some details of the Earth-Moon relationship. Goddard began working on a liquid-propellant rocket the same year.

head of its time that Goddard endured much
idicule, especially from the press. He avoided
ublicity from that moment on.

LIQUID SUCCESS

Like Tsiolkovsky, Goddard set his sights on space.
He also realized by 1909 that only liquid-propellant
ockets could produce the thrust powerful enough
or use as launch vehicles. He began designing and
esting liquid rockets in about 1924. Two years later,
e performed the first liquid-propellant test flight.

On March 16, 1926, Goddard set up his rocket
t his Aunt Effie's farm in Auburn, Massachusetts,
ear Worcester. The rocket looked like a strange
keletal device, about 11 feet (3.4 m) long. It used
eparate tanks filled with gasoline and liquid oxygen
s propellants. After ignition, the rocket rose at a
peed of about 60 miles per hour (96.5 kph) and
eached an altitude of about 41 feet (12.5 m). It
raveled a distance of 184 feet (56 m). The flight
asted only 2.5 seconds, but the event was as
ignificant to astronautics as the Wright brothers'
irst flights were to aeronautics.

Goddard continued experimenting with rockets
n Worcester, but by 1930, he realized the need
or a larger open area in which to test his rockets.

> In the history of rocketry, Dr. Robert H. Goddard
> has no peers. He was first. He was ahead of
> everyone in the design, construction, and launching
> of liquid-fuel rockets, which eventually paved the
> way into space. When Dr. Goddard did his greatest
> work, all of us who were to come later in the
> rocket and space business were still in knee pants.
> **Wernher von Braun, speaking before the
> Committee of Aeronautical and Space
> Sciences of the U.S. Senate, March 1970.**

▼ Robert Goddard poses with his liquid-propellant rocket
moments before launch on March 16, 1926. His wife
Esther took the photograph. Tanks of liquid oxygen and
gasoline at the rocket's base provided power.

He moved to Roswell, New Mexico, and launched
his first rocket there in December 1930. It reached
a height of more than 2,000 feet (600 m) and
attained a speed of 500 miles per hour (800 kph)—
much faster than the airplanes of the day.

Goddard continued improving rocket designs
at Roswell through the 1930s. His last rocket test
occurred in July 1941, four years before his death
from throat cancer. By then, some of his rockets
had traveled at more than 700 miles per hour
(1,200 kph) and reached altitudes of more than
1.5 miles (2.5 km).

CHAPTER TWO

FROM V-2s TO ICBMs

While Robert Goddard developed rockets in the United States, enthusiasts across the Atlantic Ocean in Germany also experimented with building and launching rockets. In 1942, a German army team launched the V-2 rocket— the missile that became the direct ancestor of the space launch vehicles.

Hermann Oberth's book, *The Rocket into Interplanetary Space* (1923), triggered Germany's interest in rocketry. Oberth, who also became fascinated with space travel after reading Jules Verne, discussed the practicality of rocket flights in space and suggested suitable rocket designs in his book.

In 1927, Oberth and a number of like-minded enthusiasts formed the *VfR*, or *Verein für Raumschiffahrt* ("Society for Space Travel"), based at Breslau, Germany. Within two years, the VfR had nearly nine hundred members. In 1930, its headquarters moved to Berlin, and members began using an abandoned suburban army base they called *Raketenflugplatz*, or the "rocket flying field," for their rocket experiments.

ENTER VON BRAUN

Also in 1930, eighteen-year-old Wernher von Braun joined the VfR. He soon became involved in setting up and firing experimental rockets. In July 1932,

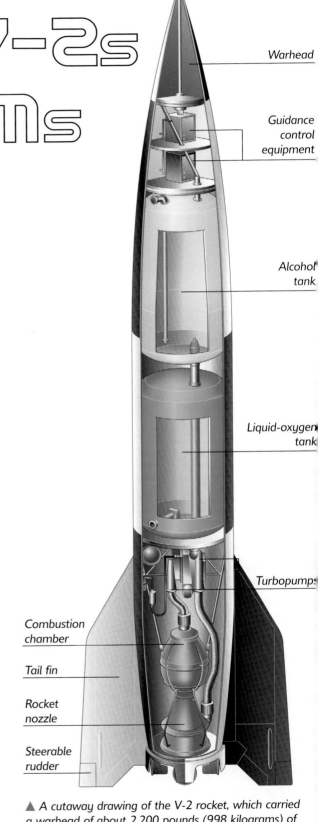

Nose fuse

Warhead

Guidance control equipment

Alcohol tank

Liquid-oxygen tank

Turbopumps

Combustion chamber

Tail fin

Rocket nozzle

Steerable rudder

▲ *A cutaway drawing of the V-2 rocket, which carried a warhead of about 2,200 pounds (998 kilograms) of explosives. Rudders on the tail fins controlled its flight.*

the VfR demonstrated one of its Repulsor rockets to the German army at nearby Kummersdorf. In October of that year, von Braun joined the army rocket research group, headed by Captain Walter Dornberger. The group worked on the development of liquid-propellant rockets.

Within a few months, von Braun and his team devised a rocket using ethanol (alcohol) and liquid oxygen as propellants. On its first flight, the rocket, known as A-1 ("*Aggregat-1*"), exploded. The army team then designed an improved A-2, which made two successful flights in 1934.

Next came the A-3, with a more powerful engine and a gyro-controlled guidance system. Its first test flight occurred in 1937, by which time von Braun and his researchers worked from a top-secret base at Peenemünde on an offshore island in the Baltic Sea. There, they also drew up plans for the A-4 rocket for use as an artillery weapon.

In October 1942—after unsuccessful launches in March and August—the A-4 performed perfectly during a test flight. The rocket followed its planned trajectory (flight path) and landed about 120 miles (190 km) away.

THE A-4 BECOMES THE V-2

By the time the A-4 made its first successful flight, World War II (1939–1945) was well underway. In July of 1943, German *Führer* Adolf Hitler ordered that production of the A-4 receive high priority. It became his *Vergeltungswaffe-zwei* ("second revenge weapon," or "V-2"), which he hoped to use to turn the tide of the war in Germany's favor.

(Hitler's first "revenge weapon," the V-1, was a flying bomb powered by a pulse jet. They called it the "buzz bomb" in Britain because of the distinctive noise it made when falling to Earth.)

▲ A V-2 rocket is hoisted onto a static test rig at White Sands Proving Ground in New Mexico in 1947. The U.S. Army fired more than sixty V-2s during tests at White Sands after World War II (WWII).

It was an unforgettable sight. In the full glare of the sunlight the rocket rose higher and higher. The flame darting from the stern was almost as long as the rocket itself. The fiery jet of gas was clear and self-contained. The rocket kept on its course as though running on rails.
Walter Dornberger, after the first successful launch of the V-2 rocket, October 1942.

In August 1943, British planes bombed Peenemünde and destroyed its rocket-producing facilities. Germany switched production of the V-2 to an underground factory known as Mittelwerk in the Harz Mountains. In September 1944, the Germans launched V-2s against targets in Paris, France, London, England, and Antwerp, Belgium.

The V-2 became the most terrifying weapon yet devised. It traveled at about 3,000 miles per hour (5,000 kph), dropped soundlessly out of the sky, and carried a 2,200-pound (998-kilogram) warhead. Germany fired more than four thousand V-2s during WWII, and most of the deadly rockets reached their targets. V-2 missiles killed more than 2,500 people in England alone.

SURRENDER

By the spring of 1945, the German army was in retreat and all V-2 operations had ceased. Hitler committed suicide on April 30, 1945. On May 2, von Braun and members of his rocket team surrendered to advancing U.S. forces. Five days later, the war in Europe ended.

By autumn 1945, von Braun and many engineers from his original team were in Fort Bliss, Texas. There, they began assembling V-2s from crates of parts confiscated by Allied troops and shipped to the U.S. from Germany. Rocket testing occurred at a new test facility nearby named the White Sands Proving Ground in New Mexico. Over the next few years, von Braun's team successfully launched more than sixty V-2s, many of which carried instruments that investigated the upper atmosphere.

In May 1948, they launched a modified V-2, the first two-stage rocket known as Bumper. It contained a small rocket that fired after the V-2 carried it high into the air.

▼ *Workers clear the devastation caused by a deadly V-2 bomb that hit London in 1945. The silent V-2s traveled faster than the speed of sound and fell out of the sky without warning.*

▼ The flight of a three-stage rocket, or launch vehicle. The first stage fires to lift the entire rocket assembly from the launchpad, then separates and falls away. The second stage now fires and separates. Then the third stage fires. The launch vehicle becomes progressively lighter and faster as each stage separates.

Third stage fires

Second stage falls away

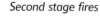

Second stage fires

First stage falls away

First stage fires

THE STEP ROCKET

The Bumper rocket served as the forerunner of the type of vehicles needed for space launches. These early step rockets consisted of two rocket units linked together. A century earlier, Konstantin Tsiolkovsky realized that only a step rocket could launch objects into space. Today's launch vehicles consist of three or more rocket units, or stages. Each stage, from the bottom up, fires to boost the stages above it to a higher speed, then falls away. Then the next stage fires, driving the now lighter vehicle to still higher speeds and altitudes.

► Camera crews record a Bumper rocket launch from the new testing facility at Cape Canaveral, Florida, on July 24, 1950. The two-stage rocket has a V-2 lower stage and a WAC Corporal upper stage. (WAC stands for "without any control.")

On the fifth Bumper launch in February 1949, the upper rocket reached a record altitude of 244 miles (393 km). The last two Bumper launches took place at a new facility in Cape Canaveral, Florida. "The Cape" soon became the focus of the United States' race into space.

THE COLD WAR

During World War II, the United States and other Western powers forged an uneasy alliance with the Soviet Union to defeat Hitler's Germany. Afterward, relations between the West and Eastern Bloc countries worsened dramatically. A Cold War began in which the two sides vied for world leadership, without resorting to "hot" or actual war. The Cold War also developed into a worldwide struggle between two different political and economic systems—capitalism in the West and communism in the East. Propaganda became an important tool in the war, with each side seeking to put a positive spin on their ideas and achievements. In the event of an actual war breaking out, both the United States and the Soviet Union began amassing a formidable arsenals of weapons— in particular, nuclear missiles. Like the V-2, nuclear weapons, nowadays classified as weapons of mass destruction (WMD), were ballistic missiles—rockets provided power until they reached a certain altitude. Then the weapons continued traveling across vast distances without power while following a ballistic trajectory, or arc, before falling on their target.

REDSTONE AND ATLAS

In 1950, von Braun's team moved to Huntsville, Alabama, and began working on the Redstone Arsenal, including the medium range—200 miles (320 km)—ballistic missiles (MRBM). These were souped-up V-2s powered by alcohol and liquid oxygen

▲ The first Redstone rocket lifts off the launchpad at Cape Canaveral, Florida, on August 20, 1953. Redstone rockets were deployed in Germany as part of the NATO (North Atlantic Treaty Organization) defense in 1958.

propellants. The first Redstone lifted off from Cape Canaveral in August 1953. A similar rocket launched the first U.S. astronauts into space eight years later.

Von Braun's team also designed the Jupiter IRBM (intermediate range ballistic missile) and the Jupiter C rockets for testing IRBMs and ICBMs (intercontinental ballistic missiles). During that time, the U.S. Air Force also developed ballistic missiles, including the Atlas ICBM and the Thor IRBM. Both types of missiles subsequently played a part in the American push into space.

▶ The United States conducts the first hydrogen bomb test on Eniwetok in the Marshall Islands in the Pacific Ocean in November 1952. Within minutes, the mushroom cloud measures 50 miles (80 km) across. No target is safe from this terrifying new rocket-launched weapon. The realization that such weapons existed heightened the fear that gripped both superpowers during the Cold War. Neither side ever used nuclear weapons against the other

"From Stettin in the Baltic to Trieste in the Adriatic, an iron curtain has descended across the Continent (of Europe). Behind that line lie all the capitals of the ancient states of central and eastern Europe. Warsaw, Berlin, Prague, Vienna, Budapest, Belgrade, Bucharest, and Sofia; all these famous cities and the populations around them lie in what I must call the Soviet sphere. . . . In a great number of countries, far from the Russian frontiers . . . the communist parties and fifth columns constitute a growing challenge and peril to Christian civilization."

Extract from British Prime Minister Winston Churchill's speech at Westminster College, Fulton, Missouri, on March 5, 1946, which coined the phrase the "Iron Curtain."

▶ *Winston Churchill delivering his speech at Westminster College, Fulton. He led Great Britain during World War II.*

CHAPTER THREE

BIRTH OF THE SPACE AGE

In 1955, President Eisenhower announced that the United States would launch an artificial satellite around Earth as part of its contribution to the 1957–1958 International Geophysical Year (IGY). The United States planned to become the first nation in space. But the Soviet Union got there first.

The U.S. had to choose between two rockets to launch its satellite: the navy's Vanguard launch vehicle or the one favored by von Braun's team, the Juno 1—a Jupiter C rocket with an extra upper stage. Vanguard was a navy project that used a launch vehicle based on the Viking and Aerobee high-altitude sounding rockets. (Sounding rockets are launched to "sound," or investigate, atmospheric conditions.) Vanguard won out. Successful test flights on Vanguard equipment in December 1956 and March 1957 encouraged the belief that the U.S. would indeed launch the first Earth satellite.

▼ *The 250-foot (76-m) dish of the radio telescope at the Jodrell Bank Radio Observatory, in Cheshire, England, came into operation in 1957. It picked up signals from Sputnik.*

OUT EAST

In July 1955, President Eisenhower announced the intention of putting a U.S. satellite into orbit. Meanwhile, the Soviet Union also raced for space. Both the Soviets and the Americans believed that whoever got there first won a propaganda victory in the "battle" for influence around the world.

Soviet rocketry development over the previous decade paralleled that of the United States. Like the Americans, Soviet forces transferred a number of German rocket experts and V-2 parts to their homeland after the end of World War II. Under the direction of Sergei Korolev, the Soviets launched their first V-2s in 1947 from Kapustin Yar, a remote site near Volvograd. There, Korolev also developed new and more powerful rockets for ballistic missiles.

By 1957, spurred on by the belligerent and all-powerful First Secretary of the Communist Party, Nikita Khrushchev, the Soviet rocket team produced the SS-6, the world's first ICBM. The SS-6 made its debut in August, traveling a distance of more than 4,000 miles (6,500 km). Western powers code-named the missile "Sapwood."

THE FIRST SPUTNIK

The Soviets launched the SS-6 from the Baikonur Cosmodrome, a new launch site in Tyuratam, Kazakhstan. On October 4, 1957, a second SS-6 stood ready for launch. This rocket carried an aluminum sphere called *Sputnik.*

At about midnight local time, the rocket's engines fired with a mighty roar. It thundered into the sky and vanished from sight, heading for orbit a minimum of 142 miles above Earth. Beeping radio signals heard around the world announced its presence. *Sputnik*, named for the Russian word for "fellow traveler," shocked the world. Fear gripped

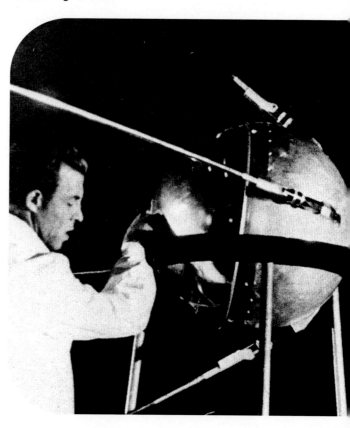

▼ A technician puts the finishing touches to Sputnik before launch. It was an aluminum globe 23 inches (58 centimeters) in diameter, fitted with antennas to transmit signals from its radio transmitter. Launched into orbit on October 4, 1957, it fell back to Earth on January 4, 1958.

citizens of the Western world when they realized that the Soviets bested the United States with this technological triumph.

> Today we have witnessed the realization of a dream nurtured by some of the finest men who ever lived, including our outstanding scientist Konstantin Eduardovich Tsiolkovsky. Tsiolkovsky brilliantly foretold that mankind would not forever remain on the Earth. The *Sputnik* is the first confirmation of his prophecy. The conquest of space has begun.
>
> **Sergei Korolev after the launch of *Sputnik* in 1957.**

SPACE DOG LAIKA

The launch of *Sputnik* delighted Khrushchev but surprised and dismayed U.S. rocket teams and the American public. *Sputnik* had a mass of 184 pounds (83 kg), much heavier than the satellites the U.S. teams were planning.

Within a week of *Sputnik*'s launch, the Soviet newspaper *Pravda* announced that a new sputnik satellite would carry an animal. On November 3, 1957, *Sputnik 2* rose into orbit with a dog named *Laika*. (Russian for "barker.") *Sputnik 2* had a mass of more than one-half ton (more than 500 kg).

The great acceleration of blasting off makes a passenger feel many times heavier than usual. Laika, a veteran of rocket tests, traveled in a pressurized capsule. Signals returned from her craft showed that she appeared unharmed despite the high-gravity forces created during liftoff. Laika also did not appear unduly affected by the weightlessness of orbit.

▼ *Space dog Laika rests in the capsule of* Sputnik 2 *before being launched into orbit on November 3, 1957. Sensors attached to Laika's body radioed back basic information about her biological condition.*

A–OK

The ICBM SS-6, or Sapwood, became the basic vehicle used by the Soviet Union for launching a variety of payloads into space. Designated A, A-1, or A-2 for space launchings, the A-1s and A-2s also included extra upper stages. The A vehicle used to launch *Sputniks* 1 and 2 had a center stage ("sustainer") with four massive boosters attached to the base. The boosters fell away after about two minutes. The main stage and boosters burned kerosene and liquid oxygen as propellants. Old but reliable technology, the A-series vehicles are still used today for launching Soyuz spacecraft that service the space shuttle.

Unfortunately, it was a one-way trip for Laika. Initially, controllers believed she died after about one week when air in her capsule ran out; a more recent examination of data indicates that she died from heat exposure shortly after reaching orbit. No matter when or how she died, the event triggered worldwide outrage from dog lovers and animal-rights proponents.

THE FLOPNIKS

U.S. rocket experts, already astonished by the mass of *Sputnik*, could hardly believe the mass of *Sputnik 2*. The Soviets clearly developed a much more powerful launching rocket than anything in the United States' possession. U.S. engineers worked frantically to catch up with the Soviet Union space successes. But the United States had yet to launch a successful satellite mission.

▶ *The Vanguard launch vehicle explodes on the launchpad on December 6, 1957, ending the first U.S. attempt to put a satellite in orbit.*

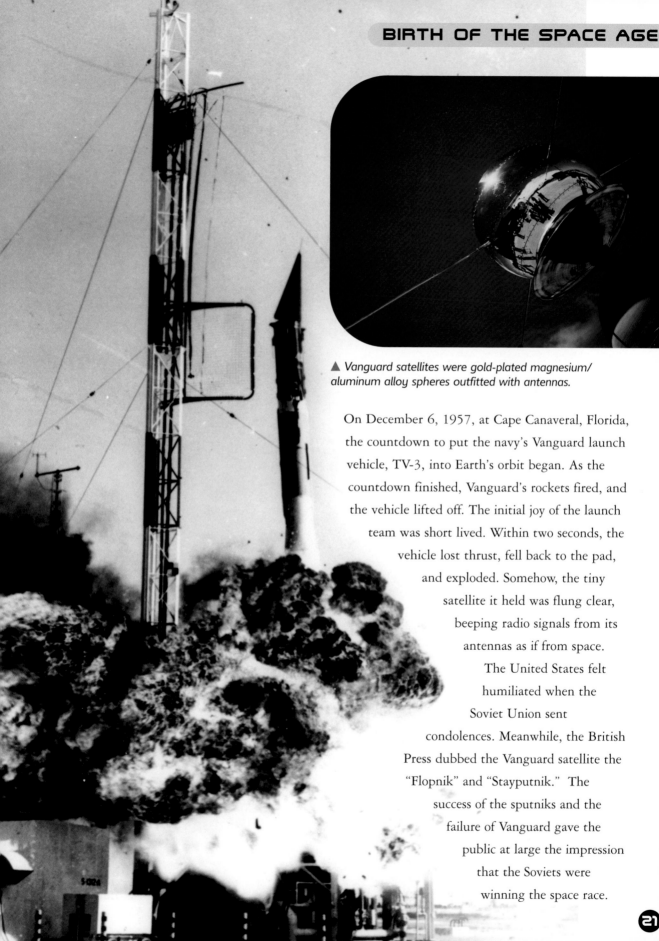

▲ *Vanguard satellites were gold-plated magnesium/ aluminum alloy spheres outfitted with antennas.*

On December 6, 1957, at Cape Canaveral, Florida, the countdown to put the navy's Vanguard launch vehicle, TV-3, into Earth's orbit began. As the countdown finished, Vanguard's rockets fired, and the vehicle lifted off. The initial joy of the launch team was short lived. Within two seconds, the vehicle lost thrust, fell back to the pad, and exploded. Somehow, the tiny satellite it held was flung clear, beeping radio signals from its antennas as if from space. The United States felt humiliated when the Soviet Union sent condolences. Meanwhile, the British Press dubbed the Vanguard satellite the "Flopnik" and "Stayputnik." The success of the sputniks and the failure of Vanguard gave the public at large the impression that the Soviets were winning the space race.

▲ *Technicians install* Explorer 1 *and the attached fourth stage rocket in the* Juno 1 *launch vehicle. The satellite and rocket together measure 81 inches (205 cm).*

But things were not that simple and easy for the Soviets. They conducted their space program in secret and never released details of any failures, such as the explosion on the launchpad of the first SS-6 missile in June 1957. The United States, on the other hand, conducted its space program in the open, so the public witnessed all of its failures as well as successes.

SUCCESS AT LAST

Fortunately for the United States, a month before the Vanguard failure, von Braun's team got the go-ahead to launch a satellite using the Jupiter C variant, Juno 1. This rocket used a liquid propellant for its first stage and three other stages of solid rocket fuel.

The first launch attempt came on January 31, 1958. The launch went perfectly, and the fourth stage, with the satellite attached, achieved orbit as planned. The satellite was aptly named *Explorer 1* because it began exploring space around Earth for the first time.

JAMES VAN ALLEN (b. 1914)

James Alfred Van Allen, who devised the radiation experiments on the *Explorer 1* and *Explorer 3* (March 1958) satellites, was born at Mount Pleasant, Iowa. He began specializing in high-altitude research after World War II, developing instruments for V-2 rockets. Van Allen returned to the University of Iowa in 1951 as professor of physics. He designed instruments for many space probes, including the groundbreaking *Mariner 2* to Venus, *Mariner 4* to Mars, and *Pioneers 10* and *11* to Jupiter.

▶ *James Van Allen (middle) celebrates the successful launch of* Explorer 1 *with Wernher von Braun (right) and William Pickering (left). Von Braun led the army team that built the launch vehicle; Pickering was Director of the Jet Propulsion Laboratory, which built the satellite.*

Explorer 1 measured about 3 feet (1 m) long and had a mass of about 10.5 pounds (5 kg). Its battery-powered instruments included a Geiger counter to measure the radiation in space. It also carried a miniature tape recorder that relayed data to ground stations scattered around the world.

EXPLORER'S DISCOVERY

Explorer 1 carried miniaturized lightweight components, making it technically more advanced than the Sputniks. Its Geiger counter made the first major discovery in space when it detected bands of intense radiation (electrically charged solar particles trapped by Earth's magnetic field) at about 600 miles (960 km) above Earth. These bands were named the Van Allen radiation belts for the scientist who devised the experiment, James A. Van Allen.

THE GRAPEFRUIT SATELLITE

On February 5, 1958, the navy attempted another Vanguard launch, which failed. On March 5, von Braun's team attempted another Juno 1 launch, which also failed. But on March 17, the navy scored its first success and launched a tiny sphere called *Vanguard 1* into orbit. It was the first satellite powered by solar cells.

At about 5 inches (16 cm) across and a weight of only 3 pounds (1.5 kg), *Vanguard 1* is also the smallest satellite ever launched. Soviet leader Khrushchev dismissed it as a "mere grapefruit."

The Soviet Union backed up his remark by launching *Sputnik 3* in May. It measured 11.5 feet (3.5 m) long and weighed 1.5 tons (1.3 tonnes).

▶ Juno 1 *lifts off the launchpad at Cape Canaveral on January 31, 1958. Within minutes, it places the first U.S. satellite* Explorer 1 *into orbit.* Explorer 1 *transmits information about the Earth's radiation belts until May 23.*

CHAPTER FOUR

PIONEERING SPACE TRAVEL

Space-dog Laika's flight on *Sputnik 2* in November 1957 indicated that the Soviet Union hoped to maintain its lead in space exploration. The United States lagged behind, with its first successful launch of a U.S. space vehicle finally occurring in January 1958. Later that year, the United States announced its man-in-space program.

The National Aeronautics and Space Administration (NASA) became an official government entity on October 1, 1958. Part of the National Aeronautics and Space Act, it provided for "research into the problems of flight within and outside the Earth's atmosphere, and for other purposes." President Eisenhower signed the law that created NASA in July of that year, keeping in mind the Cold War intent of challenging the Soviet Union for supremacy in space exploration.

NACA MERGER

The National Advisory Committee for Aeronautics (NACA), formed in 1915 to promote U.S. research into aeronautics and aviation, always functioned at the cutting edge of technology. When it became NASA in 1958, the new organization integrated the operations of NACA and concentrated on spaceflight.

NACA facilities that transferred to NASA's authority included Langley Memorial Aeronautical Laboratory (renamed Langley Research Center) in Hampton, Virginia, and the High-Speed Flight Station (renamed Dryden Flight Research Center) at Edwards Air Force Base, California. NASA also

▶ The original "blue meatball" NASA insignia, designed in 1959, features silver letters on a dark blue background with stars representing space. The ellipse depicts orbital flight. The red vector represents NASA's trajectory and direction toward the stars and outer space. In 1975, the agency switched to the red "worm" logo. NASA reverted to the blue meatball logo with an extended vector that reaches beyond the blue field of stars in 1992.

absorbed von Braun's team at the newly created Marshall Space Flight Center at Huntsville, Alabama.

The prime launch site for NASA was Cape Canaveral in Florida, operated by Marshall's Launch Operations Directorate. In 1962, NASA extended its facilities onto the adjacent Merritt Island—the future launch site for the upcoming Apollo Moon missions. After the tragic assassination of President Kennedy in 1963, NASA renamed the launch area Cape Kennedy and the entire area the Kennedy Space Center.

MERCURY TAKES SHAPE

NASA's first administrator, Keith Glennan,
announced the U.S. man-in-space program on
October 7, 1958 and Project Mercury in December.
By then, detailed plans for launching Mercury
astronauts were already set. Each astronaut would
fly into space inside a pressurized capsule atop a
modified missile, such as a Redstone or an Atlas.

Maxime Faget, a member of the NASA team at
Langley, designed the bell-shaped Mercury capsule.
Retrorockets on the capsules could help reduce its
speed as it dropped back to Earth. As it reentered
the atmosphere (blunt-end first), the capsule's heat
shield protected it and the astronaut inside from the
extreme temperatures that resulted from the
friction of the speeding capsule against the

▲ The "Original Seven" astronauts selected for the
Mercury program. Left to right: front row—Walter
"Wally" Schirra, Donald "Deke" Slayton, John Glenn Jr.,
and M. Scott Carpenter; back row—Alan B. Shepard Jr.,
Virgil "Gus" Grissom, and L. Gordon Cooper.

▼ The Vehicle Assembly Building (VAB) under
construction on Merritt Island, near Cape Canaveral,
Florida. Preparation of the site began in November 1962.
The building was completed in June 1965. Originally
designed for Saturn V Moon rocket assembly, the VAB
was later modified to prepare space shuttles for launch.

▲ *In the early 1960s, the launchpads at Cape Canaveral, Florida, were used for test-firing ICBMs. Rocket launches at the Cape began in 1950. This facility is now called the Eastern Test Range.*

atmosphere. The heat shield prevented the capsule and its passengers from burning up before the returning spacecraft splashed down in the ocean.

NASA considered but rejected alternative methods of launching astronauts. One proposal involved a boost-glide concept, in which a rocket would boost into space the astronaut and his flying machine (a modified X-15 rocket plane), which would then glide back to Earth (*see page 32*). Another suggested design resembled the spherical capsules like the ones the Soviets used.

LANDING ON THE STEPPES

Unknown to the United States, Soviet space scientists chose a spherical capsule named *Vostok* ("East") for their first manned spacecraft. A powerful booster rocket derived from the SS-6 ICBM served as the launch vehicle.

Vostok's second section contained various instruments and retrorockets. Before reentry, it would separate from the crew capsule, which would parachute back to Earth on its own and land on the ground. Soviet cosmonauts always returned to Earth in spherical capsules that made ground landings in the Soviet steppes area.

TOWARD SATURN

After von Braun and his team transferred to the Marshall Space Flight Center at Huntsville in 1960, they concentrated on developing powerful heavy-lift launch vehicles called Saturn. The first design, Saturn 1, consisting of eight engines in a cluster, made its first flight in October 1961. By then, the Apollo Moon-landing program was underway, and the development of the Saturn launch-vehicle series was a matter of government urgency. Even so, the mighty Saturn V rocket didn't make its first flight until six years later.

COPING WITH SPACEFLIGHT

NASA engineers designed the first U.S. manned spacecraft (Mercury) so that Mission Control could fly them automatically from the ground; there was no real need for the astronauts to be ace test pilots—but that's exactly what they were.

▲ Wernher von Braun stands in front of one of the Saturn heavy launch vehicles his team developed at the Marshall Space Flight Center (MSFC) in Huntsville, Alabama. Von Braun served as director of MSFC from July 1960 to February 1970.

SERGEI KOROLEV (1907–1966)

Sergei Pavlovich Korolev, referred to as simply the "Chief Designer" for many years, became the driving force behind the Soviet push into space. His obsession with rocketry began in the early 1930s, when he directed a group that built and tested liquid-propellant rockets. During World War II, he helped develop rockets for airplanes. Afterward, he headed the teams that fired V-2s and developed them into practical missiles. But his real dream was to conquer space. He helped do just that by developing the hardware—the powerful A series rockets—that sent the first sputniks into orbit, the first humans into space, and the first probes to the Moon.

▶ In July 1954, Soviet "Chief Designer" Sergei Korolev holds a dog that just completed a flight in a research rocket.

In the days before manned flights, no one knew how, or even if, humans could function in space. Could they cope with the fierce G-forces during launch and the equally fierce forces caused by severe braking during reentry? How would the human body handle weightlessness? Space engineers could not take chances and designed automatically controlled spacecraft. They also flew test flights with animals aboard.

HIGH FLIERS

Animals preceded humans into space in both the Soviet and American space programs. While the United States favored using primates—monkeys and chimpanzees—the Soviet scientists used dogs.

In 1949, Korolev's team at Kapustin Yar began launching dogs in the nose cones of Pobeda ("Victory") missiles, developed from the V-2. Sometimes they traveled in pressurized cabins and sometimes they wore space suits and helmets. Cameras filmed their reactions.

LITTLE ARROW AND SQUIRREL

Laika is the best-known space pioneering dog, but when she flew into space in 1957 (*see page 20*), the technology to recover her from orbit did not exist. By 1960, plans for the safe launch and recovery of a space capsule were nearly complete. On August 19, the Soviets tested the Vostok capsule design. The *Korabl-Sputnik 2*, often called *Sputnik 5*, contained two huskies named Strelka ("Little Arrow") and Belka ("Squirrel"). Rats, mice, insects, plants, and seeds traveled with the dogs in a pressurized "ark." A TV camera photographed their reactions and returned images to Earth. A day later, the so-called ark made a perfect parachute landing, its precious cargo alive and well—proving that living things could survive the perils of spaceflight. Radio Moscow announced afterward: "Practical

▼ A Saturn I launch vehicle in the "Rocket Park" at the Kennedy Space Center's Visitor Center clearly shows the rocket cluster that made up the vehicle's first stage. NASA workers sometimes referred to this Saturn I rocket as "cluster's last stand."

▲ A Little Joe rocket blasts off the launchpad. These rockets tested Mercury spacecraft and its escape tower on top. The tower was designed to lift the capsule clear of the launch rocket if an emergency arose during liftoff. Little Joe rockets also carried animal astronauts on brief flights (see page 30).

possibilities are now being created for man's flight into outer space." Three more dog flights followed. *Sputnik 6* failed, burning up in the atmosphere on reentry. But the next two missions, *Sputnik*s 9 and 10 in March 1961, went perfectly. The first manned flight could not be far away—and it wasn't.

On April 12, 1961, Soviet pilot and cosmonaut Yuri Gagarin blasted off from the Baikonur Cosmodrome in Kazakhstan and climbed into orbit. He orbited the Earth once in his *Vostok 1* capsule.

Only 108 minutes after liftoff, Gagarin returned

safely to Earth. "I could have gone on flying through space forever," he said. The Soviets kept their space-race lead with Gherman Titov's flight on August 6, 1961. His incredible (back then) *Vostok 2* mission lasted a little longer than a day.

MONKEY BUSINESS

The United States trained its animal astronauts at the Aeromedical Field Laboratory at Holloman Air Force Base in New Mexico. They maintained a veritable zoo there, including not only monkeys and chimpanzees, but also hogs and bears.

The U.S. planned suborbital spaceflights for its first manned space missions. A capsule launched by a rocket to high altitude (but not into orbit) would return to Earth via a ballistic trajectory.

NASA launched several primates on suborbital test flights. In December 1958, a squirrel monkey named Gordo was launched by a Jupiter booster. Although Gordo survived the flight well, his nose cone (capsule) sank in the ocean upon landing. A similar flight in May 1959 ended on a happier note. The *Bioflight 2* capsule contained a rhesus monkey named Able and a squirrel monkey named Miss Baker. They stood up to their brief spaceflight well and were recovered safely.

▲ The squirrel monkey Miss Baker sits next to a ball at the Alabama Space and Rocket Center at Huntsville in 1981, twenty-two years after her June 1959 flight in the nose cone of a Jupiter rocket.

▲ Launch of chimpanzee Ham in a Mercury spacecraft on January 31, 1961. The spacecraft rose to a height of about 155 miles (250 km) and splashed down successfully 420 miles (675 km) downrange.

MERCURY FLIGHTS

On January 31, 1961, a Mercury-Redstone-type launch vehicle that would soon launch the first U.S. astronaut into space blasted off from Cape Canaveral carrying a chimpanzee named Ham. During the flight, the chimp performed a set of simple tasks that involved pulling levers. Despite experiencing a reentry braking force of 15 Gs— fifteen times the normal pull of gravity—Ham suffered no ill effects from the experience. (But he made it clear to his handlers that he didn't want to get back into the capsule to fly in space again!)

Ham's brief flight tested the capsule design used by the "Original 7" ("Mercury 7") astronauts. Each of those men chose the name for his capsule. All six names for capsules that flew in the Mercury program ended with the numeral seven—representing the team of seven astronauts with the "right stuff."

On May 5, 1961, three weeks after Gagarin's pioneering flight, Alan Shepard became the first U.S astronaut in space when he lifted off from Cape Canaveral in the *Freedom 7* Mercury capsule. Shepard's suborbital flight, just like Ham's, was brief—a little more than fifteen minutes—but it provided a human space-race victory for the United States. In July, Mercury astronaut Virgil "Gus" Grissom made a nearly identical fifteen-minute suborbital flight in his *Liberty Bell 7* capsule, which nearly sank in the Atlantic after splashdown when a hatch blew open unexpectedly. A navy helicopter rescued Grissom just in time.

Near the end of November 1961, chimpanzee Enos blasted off the launchpad and climbed into orbit. He circled Earth twice before returning safely.

The Mercury capsule and Atlas booster used to attain Earth orbit worked together perfectly. They cleared the way for humans to follow—which is what John Glenn Jr. did on February 20, 1962. Riding in the Mercury capsule *Friendship 7*, Glenn spent a little less than five hours in space. He orbited the Earth three times before touching down safely.

In all, six of the seven Mercury astronauts flew missions before NASA cancelled the program.

> You wonder why I use hogs and chimpanzees? Well, man is somewhere between the hog and the chimpanzee. Some people are more like hogs; others more like chimpanzees.
> **Colonel John P. Stapp, Holloman Aeromedical Field Laboratory, New Mexico.**

▶ *After his successful flight, Ham shakes hands with Commander Ralph A. Brackett of the USS* Donner.

THE X-PLANES

The Mercury method of launching astronauts—on top of a missile inside a container (capsule)—was chosen to get a U.S. astronaut into orbit as soon as possible. An alternative rocket launched and propelled space plane had also been considered.

A prototype space plane, the X-15, already existed by October 1958. Designed for an air-launch from a high-flying aircraft, its rocket motors would then ignite, boosting it to the atmosphere's outer fringes. Afterward, it would descend and land.

The X-15 was designed to investigate high-speed, high-altitude flight. It measured 50 feet (15 m) long and had a wingspan of 22 feet (6.7 m),

▲ *Dryden test pilot Neil Armstrong poses with the first X-15 rocket plane after a successful flight on January 1, 1960. Nine and a half years later, he would achieve fame as the first man on the Moon. Armstrong's X-15 is now on display at the National Air and Space Museum in Washington, D.C.*

with an outer skin of nickel-steel alloy over a frame of titanium and stainless steel. These heat-resistant materials allowed the aircraft to survive severe aerodynamic heating—heating because of air friction—when traveling at very high speeds.

AT DRYDEN

Flights of the X-15s were conducted at the Dryden Research Center at Edwards, California, in the

Mojave Desert. Located on the edge of Rogers Dry Lake, the area provides a wide-open flat area for test flights and landings.

The first X-15 "captive" (a larger aircraft carries the test airplane to a designated altitude before releasing it) flight tests from under the wing of a Superfortress B-52 aircraft occurred in March 1959. Test pilot Scott Crossfield made the first powered flight of an X-15 that April—the first of 199 X-15 flights that continued for many years until October 24, 1968.

During these missions, eight pilots gained their astronauts' wings by flying at an altitude of more than 50 miles (80 km). The top speed attained was 4,720 miles per hour (7,274 kph), or nearly seven times the speed of sound (Mach 7).

BEATING THE BARRIER

The Dryden Research Center was also where Captain Charles ("Chuck") Yeager became the first person to "break" the sound barrier by flying at more than the speed of sound (Mach 1). Piloting a Bell X-1 rocket plane, he produced a sonic boom on October 14, 1947. In all, three X-1s were built. They made a total of 156 flights through 1951.

▼ Because the X-15 consumed enormous quantities of fuel, a B-52 bomber carried it to an altitude of about 45,000 feet (14,000 m) before releasing, or air-launching, the test plane. The X-15's rocket engine would then ignite, and the pilot would either climb steeply to an even higher altitude or try to reach maximum speed in level flight.

CHAPTER FIVE

THE AGE OF SATELLITES

The launches of primitive satellites in the late 1950s gave way in the early 1960s to a great expansion in space activities and laid the foundations for the satellite networks that have since revolutionized our world—particularly in the fields of communications, meteorology, and navigation.

Today, a network of Intelsat communications satellites in geostationary orbit rings the globe. (In a geostationary orbit, a satellite travels at the same speed as Earth spins and so appears fixed in the same position in the sky.) This satellite network relays telephone calls, TV programs, fax messages, e-mails, and computer data around the world in seconds. But the idea of such a network predated the Space Age. British science writer Arthur C. Clarke (who later wrote the science-fiction classic *2001, A Space Odyssey*) put forth the idea as early as 1945.

ECHO TECHNOLOGY

The last satellite placed in orbit in 1958 was a kind of communications satellite. It was an Atlas ICBM launched by the U.S. Army in Project Score (Signal Communication by Orbiting Radio Equipment). The satellite broadcast prerecorded messages, including Christmas greetings from President Eisenhower.

In May 1960, NASA conducted the first communications satellite tests using a huge balloon that inflated in orbit. Appropriately called *Echo 1*, it reflected radio signals between ground stations.

◄ *The pioneering communications satellite* Echo 1 *leaves a trail in this long-exposure photograph taken of the Milky Way in 1960.*

GETTING ACTIVE

The signals passed on by *Echo* were weak, passive signals by the time they arrived at a receiving station. A more useful communications satellite needed to actively strengthen radio signals before passing them on to another station.

The first active satellite entered launched orbit in July 1962. Named *Telstar*, it was also the first commercial satellite funded by communications giant AT&T. Ground stations for *Telstar* were located at Andover, Maine, and at sites in England and France. Just hours after launch, *Telstar* flashed its first live TV image from the United States across the Atlantic Ocean—an image of the American flag fluttering in the breeze at the Andover station.

Telstar circled in a low Earth orbit, which allowed TV communications across the Atlantic for only twenty minutes at a time. Constant satellite coverage required a geostationary orbit—as imagined by Clarke.

Syncom 3, launched in August 1964, became the first successful satellite placed in geostationary orbit

▲ *NASA's second balloon communications satellite,* Echo 2, *inflated to its full size of 135 feet (41 m) in diameter during preflight tests. It was launched in January 1964.*

22,300 miles (35,900 km) above Earth. Poised over the Equator near the International Date Line in the Pacific, *Syncom 3* broadcast the opening ceremonies of Japan's Tokyo Olympics. "Live by satellite" became the new buzzwords.

A GLOBAL NETWORK

In the same month, a group of nations established and funded a global communications network called *Intelsat* (the International Telecommunications Satellite Organization). Intelsat launched *Intelsat 1* (*Early Bird*) in April 1965.

Also that same month, the Soviets launched *Molniya 1*, the first link in its communications satellite system. Molniya satellites entered a highly elliptical, or oval, orbit that kept them over the horizon of the Soviet Union for most of the time.

◄ *Echo and Telstar satellites communicated with this unique horn antenna, built in 1959 at Bell Telephone Laboratories in Holmdel, New Jersey. In 1990, it was designated a national historic landmark.*

A WEATHER EYE

Early in the Space Age, meteorologists (scientists who study weather) realized that satellites could look down on weather systems and track them from above. They used satellites to monitor weather data and conditions anywhere in the world, including over the oceans.

The United States launched the first dedicated weather satellite in April 1960. Named *Tiros 1* (*T*elevision and *I*nfra*R*ed *O*bservation *S*atellite), it used a TV system to record cloud formations in both visible light and invisible infrared radiation. *Tiros 1* circled Earth in a polar orbit that took it over the North and South Poles, which allowed for a scan of the entire rotating Earth below.

Ten satellites in the Tiros series (1960–1965) were followed by nine ESSA (Environmental Scienc Services Administration) series (1965–1968). Then the National Oceanographic and Atmospheric Administration (NOAA) began funding its own series of satellites, as it still does today.

AIDING NAVIGATION

Other global satellite networks revolutionized navigation, providing for precision location on land

▼ *Weather satellites image cloud systems over vast regions at regular intervals, which increases the accuracy of meteorological forecasting.*

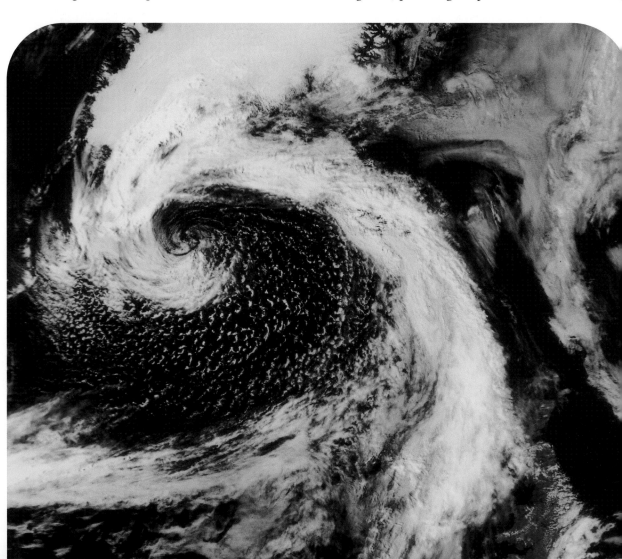

ea, and in the air. The first navigation satellites eveloped by the U.S. military provided accurate fixes" of Polaris nuclear submarines.

The *Transit 1B*, launched in April 1960 as part f the Transit System, became operational two years ter. The Transit System remained classified (secret) ntil 1967, when its navigation systems became vailable for civilian use. Also that year, the Soviet Jnion launched its first Transit-type satellite, which ter led to an operational navigation system.

Transits remained in use until the 1990s, when ne present Global Positioning System (GPS) took ver. The GPS operates with a network of twenty- our Navstar satellites in various orbits. GPS eceivers automatically calculate their position from ery precise time and position signals transmitted om the system's satellites. By getting a "fix" on everal satellites, the receiver pinpoints its position o within a few yards (meters). Russia has a similar etwork, known as *Glonass* (*Glo*bal *na*vigation atellite *system*).

A Landsat 1 *image of the San Francisco Bay area. aunched in 1972, Landsat 1 was the first dedicated emote-sensing satellite—one that pictures Earth's surface om orbit using different wavelengths (colors) of light.*

▼ *A British-built Ariel satellite blasts off from the NASA launch site on Wallops Island off the coast of Virginia. Both the United States and Russia regularly launch satellites for other countries.*

SPACE GOES INTERNATIONAL

As the United States and the Soviet Union gradually mastered the art of launching satellites, other countries pursued their own space programs. In 1962—in the first example of international cooperation in space—a U.S. Thor-Delta launch vehicle boosted Britain's first satellite, *Ariel 1*, into orbit. Three years later, France used its own launch vehicle to loft its first satellite, *Asterix 1*, into orbit, thus becoming the world's third independent space power. Japan became the fourth in 1970, when it launched *Ohsumi*; and in the same year, China became the fifth with *China 1*—notable for broadcasting music entitled "The East is Red." In 1971, Britain joined the space powers when it launched *Prospero* with its Black Arrow launch vehicle from Woomera, Australia. India followed with *Rohini 1B* in 1980, and Israel launched its first satellite, *Offeq 1*, in 1988.

ORBITS

Satellites follow a variety of different-shaped paths
in space as they orbit Earth. Some satellites orbit
in a huge circle, but most follow an elliptical, or
oval, path. An equatorial orbit—directly above
Earth's Equator—makes a satellite appear fixed in
the sky, or "geostationary." A satellite in equatorial
orbit travels at the same speed that Earth rotates
on its axis.

SATELLITE CONSTRUCTION

Satellites come in all shapes and sizes. Because
they circle high above the atmosphere, they do not
need smooth, streamlined shapes. Engineers design
imaging, communications, or research satellites in
whatever shape best fits their function.

The less a satellite weighs, the less rocket powe
it needs to achieve orbit. Most satellites are built
from strong, lightweight materials, such as alloys
(mixtures) of aluminum, magnesium, and berylliun
Plastic reinforced with carbon fibers is light and
immensely strong, which makes it another good
material for use in satellites.

INSTRUMENTATION

Satellites carry a variety of different instruments,
depending on their use. They include equipment

▼ *This huge Applications Technology Satellite, with
a communications antenna 30 feet (9 m) in diameter,
undergoes testing in an enormous vacuum chamber at
the Johnson Space Center in the 1970s. Two panels of
solar cells visible on the trusses above the antenna
provide power for the spacecraft.*

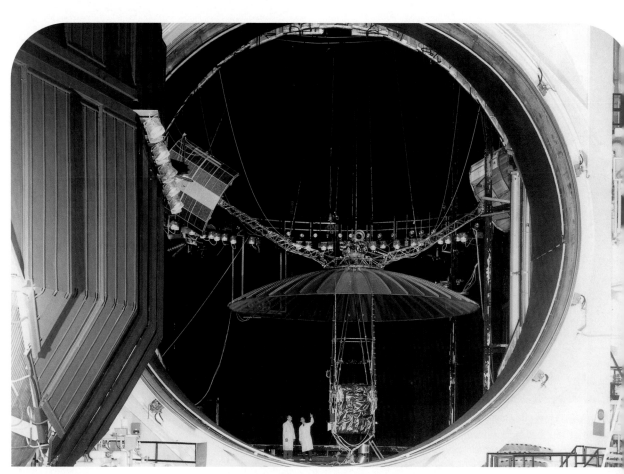

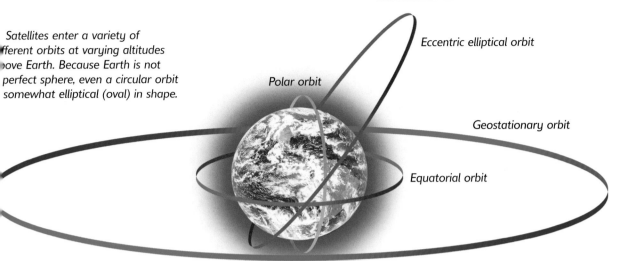

Satellites enter a variety of different orbits at varying altitudes above Earth. Because Earth is not a perfect sphere, even a circular orbit is somewhat elliptical (oval) in shape.

Eccentric elliptical orbit

Polar orbit

Geostationary orbit

Equatorial orbit

detect charged particles or measure radiation and magnetism. Satellites may carry telescopes or cameras that collect information about Earth, other celestial ("heavenly") bodies, and even space itself.

COMMUNICATIONS AND TRACKING

A satellite must communicate with Earth. It receives signals beamed up to it from ground control stations on Earth and transmits its own signals, such as weather data, back down to the stations.

The communications system includes radio transmitters and receivers, antennas, and recorders. The recorders store data from the instruments while the satellite loses contact with the ground monitors.

Ground stations use very large dish antennas to transmit and receive satellite signals. Many of these antennas swivel to track (follow) satellites as they pass overhead. Antennas that communicate with satellites in geostationary orbit remain fixed in place. Just like the fixed-position geostationary satellite high above, it stays in the same spot.

ELECTRICAL POWER

Electricity powers the radios, instruments, and recorders on satellites. Panels of solar cells harness the power of the Sun. Solar cells, made from thin wafers of silicon (similar to the microchips used in computers and other devices), convert solar energy directly into electricity.

Each solar cell produces only a tiny trickle of electricity, so solar panels must contain thousands of solar cells. The panels may form part of the body of the satellite or cover separate satellite "wings."

ATTITUDE CONTROL

A satellite's position in space is called its attitude. Since most satellites depend upon solar energy for proper operation, their solar panels must always face the Sun. Also, any cameras or sensors that study particular stars or planets must always point in a certain direction.

That means that one of the most important satellite systems is attitude control. Without the proper attitude, a satellite is a virtually useless piece of metal and wires in space, or "space junk." The attitude control system uses a number of sensors programmed to "lock on" to suitable targets, such as Earth, the Sun, or a bright star, such as the dog star, *Sirius*. The locked sensors maintain the satellite's attitude and keep it working properly.

CHAPTER SIX

THE GREAT ESCAPE

The Soviet Union and the United States had scarcely mastered the art of launching satellites into orbit when they began aiming space probes at the Moon, the planets, and beyond. Spacecraft needed to reach incredible speeds to escape the unrelenting pull of Earth's gravity. Only then could they explore deeper into space.

Launching a satellite to orbiting altitude is difficult enough. A rocket vehicle must also boost the craft to orbital velocity—a speed of 17,500 miles per hour (28,000 kph). But even in orbit, gravity still binds a spacecraft to Earth.

▼ *A sequence of four pictures taken by the lunar probe Ranger 9, seconds before it crash-landed on March 24, 1965, in the Alphonsus crater. White circles in images 1 and 2 show the point of future impact. Its cameras came online twenty minutes before the programmed crash.*

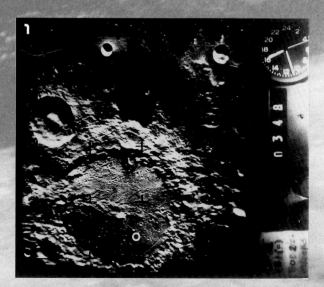

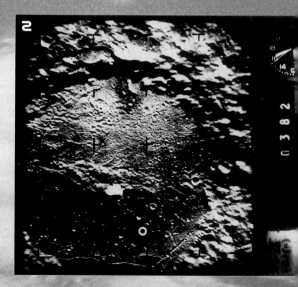

To escape completely from gravity, a spacecraft must reach escape velocity—25,000 miles per hour (40,000 kph).

After losing the race to launch the world's first satellite to the Soviet Union, U.S. space scientists aimed to win the next race by sending the first unmanned spacecraft to the Moon. They combined a Thor ICBM and stages from a Vanguard booster to create a Thor-Able launch vehicle, powerful enough to achieve the necessary escape speeds.

TO THE MOON—OR BUST

With this vehicle, they launched the first probe (*Pioneer 0*) on August 17, 1958, but it blew up at a height of 10 miles (16 km). The next three probes (*Pioneers 1, 2*, and *3*) in October, November, and December, respectively, failed when each fell back to Earth. But despite these failures, the American public became caught up in the excitement of the Space Age and the competition with the Soviets.

Once again, though, the Soviet Union used a much more powerful A-1 rocket booster (derived from the one that launched the first Sputniks) to beat the United States in the space race. The Soviet *Luna 1* (or *Lunik 1*) probe launched on January 2, 1959, aimed to hit the Moon. Instead, it made a near miss on January 4, flying past the Moon at a distance of about 3,000 miles (5,000 km).

The United States achieved some success in March 1959, when the *Pioneer 4* probe passed about 37,000 miles (60,000 km) from the surface of the Moon.

IMPACT!

On September 12, 1959, the Soviet *Luna 2* shot toward the Moon. Two days later, it scored a bull's-eye, impacting the Moon in the region between

▲ *Background image: An astronaut's view of space beyond Earth's atmosphere. The distant Moon, Earth's constant natural satellite, serves as the obvious first target for Soviet and U.S. space probes.*

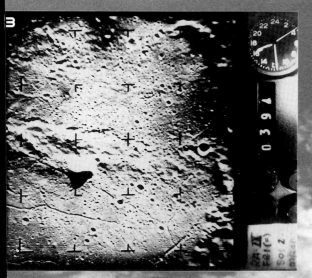

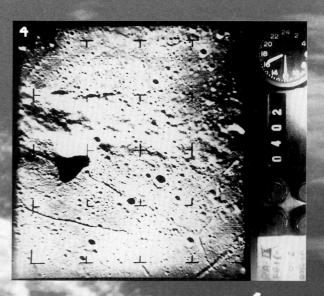

the prominent craters *Aristarchus*, *Aristillus*, and *Autolychus*. Three weeks later, the Moon-bound *Luna 3* orbited the Moon and returned to Earth. As it swung around the far side of the Moon, it took the first-ever photographs of the lunar surface that is always hidden from Earth. Those images revealed that the far side is almost entirely mountainous, with no great seas (*maria*) like the familiar side.

The United States continued trying to reach the Moon. All of its attempts throughout 1959 and 1960 to send Pioneer/Orbiter probes into lunar orbit failed. Between 1961 and 1964, the U.S. launched seven Ranger probes designed to take close-up photographs of the lunar surface before crash-landing. Of these, only the *Ranger 7* (July 1964) craft succeeded. It transmitted thousands of high-resolution pictures of the Moon's surface.

After *Ranger 7*'s success, two more successful Ranger missions occurred in 1965. *Surveyor 1* achieved a precision soft landing and relayed images for six weeks in 1966. Also in 1966, *Lunar Orbiter*s *1* and *2* went into orbit around the Moon, with the objective of taking photographs of possible landing sites for the Apollo Moon-landing missions.

PROBING THE PLANETS

The United States and the Soviet Union also faced off in the quest to reach the planets first. Earth's two nearest neighbors—Venus and Mars—were the obvious targets. But even at their closest approaches, the two planets lie more than one hundred times farther away than the Moon.

The United States launched the first successful interplanetary probe just to "sample" the conditions of interplanetary space, which were unknown at the time. *Pioneer 5* sped into space in March 1960 and sent back signals from a distance of 23 million miles

THE LURE OF MARS

Called the Red Planet for its fiery red color, Mars has intrigued people for centuries. In 1877, Italian astronomer Giovanni Schiaparelli reported seeing "canali" (channels) on Mars. This was mistranslated as "canals," or artificial waterways, causing Earthlings to imagine the existence of a race of intelligent Martians that built canals to irrigate their crops. U.S. astronomer Percival Lowell, another great believer in Martians, built the famous Lowell Observatory in Flagstaff, Arizona, to study the Red Planet.

(37 million km). It reported on the solar wind—the charged particles streaming from the Sun—and its effect on Earth's magnetic field.

THE ANCIENT MARINERS

Just as the United States struggled to reach the Moon, the Soviets struggled to reach the planets. Two Soviet attempts at Mars in 1960 failed, as did one attempt to target Venus in 1961 and four in 1962. The U.S. probe *Mariner 2* succeeded in becoming the first planetary probe in 1962, when it completed a flyby of Venus at a planned distance of nearly 22,000 miles (35,500 km). *Mariner 2* reported that Venus was scorching hot, with a thick atmosphere and no appreciable magnetic field.

Over the next two years, the Soviet Union launched a total of nine probes to Venus and Mars without success. Then the U.S. probe *Mariner 4* set out for Mars and, after an eight-month journey, returned twenty-one close-up photographs of the surface in July 1965. The images showed a barren, cratered landscape, not unlike parts of the Moon.

The Soviet Union finally succeeded in flying its *Venera 4* probe into Venus's atmosphere in 1967 and had success with similar probes later. But the United States dominated planetary exploration in the years to come.

◣ Mariner 1 *spectacularly lifts off the launchpad at Cape Canaveral on July 22, 1962, on top of an Atlas-Agena launch vehicle. It is the first attempt by the United States to send a probe to a planet—Venus. Unfortunately, the launch vehicle fails to escape Earth's gravity. But on August 27, an identical launch vehicle succeeds in sending Mariner 2 toward Venus. The probe makes its closest approach to the planet on December 14, 1962.*

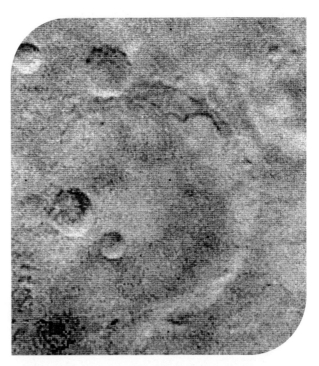

▲ *One of the best of the twenty-one images returned by* Mariner 4 *in July 1965 shows the cratered surface of Mars at a distance of about 6,000 miles (9,600 km). It also detected an atmosphere of carbon dioxide.*

1865

French novelist Jules Verne writes *From the Earth to the Moon.*

1898

English author H.G. Wells publishes *The War of the Worlds.*

1903

Konstantin Tsiolkovsky in Russia publishes first book about the principles of space flight, *Exploring Space with Reactive Devices.*

December 17: The Wright brothers, Wilbur and Orville, make the first airplane flights.

1915

The United States establishes NACA—the National Advisory Committee for Aeronautics—to promote

research into airplane flight; becomes NASA in 1958.

1923

In Munich, Germany, Hermann Oberth publishes his influential book, *The Rocket into Interplanetary Space.*

1926

March 16: In the United States, Robert Goddard builds and fires the first liquid-propellant rocket.

1927

The *VfR* (*Verein für Raumschiffahrt*) is founded in Germany and begins rocket experiments.

1930

Robert Goddard begins rocket launchings at Roswell, New Mexico.

1932

Wernher von Braun joins German army rocket team as civilian employee.

1942

October: First successful flight of the A-4 (V-2) rocket, designed by Wernher von Braun's team.

1944

September: Germany begins bombardment of London with V-2 rocket bombs.

1945

May: Wernher von Braun and members of his rocket team surrender to U.S. forces. They are flown to the United States in September.

1947

Soviet Union begin tests with V-2 rockets at Kapustin Yar.

1948

In the United States, the first launch at White Sands Proving Ground of a two-stage Bumper rocket.

1950

July: First launch of a Bumper rocket from Cape Canaveral.

1953

August: First launch of a Redstone rocket from Cape Canaveral.

1955

July: President Eisenhower announces the U.S. intention of launching a satellite during the upcoming 1957–1958 International Geophysical Year

1957

August: Soviet Union launches its first ICBM, the S-6 (called Sapwood in U.S.)

October 4: Soviet Union launches *Sputnik* to usher in the Space Age.

November 3: *Sputnik 2* is launched carrying space dog Laika.

December 6: A U.S. Vanguard launch vehicle explodes on the launchpad in the first attempt to put a satellite in orbit.

1958

January 31: First U.S. satellite *Explorer 1* launched.

October 1: NASA (National Aeronautics and Space Administration) established.

December: The U.S. manned space program is named Project Mercury.

1959

The Soviet Union launches three Luna probes to the Moon; the first just misses, the second crash lands, and the third photographs the Moon's far side.

March: First flights of the U.S. X-15 rocket plane.

1960

April: NASA launches first weather satellite (*Tiros 1*) and in May the first passive communications satellite (*Echo 1*).

August 19: Soviet Union flies two dogs (Strelka and Belka) into orbit in a Vostok capsule and recovers them safely.

Wernher von Braun becomes director of the Marshall Space Flight Center at Huntsville, Alabama.

1961

January 31: U. S. launches chimpanzee Ham on a successful suborbital flight in a Mercury capsule.

April 12: Soviet cosmonaut Yuri Gagarin becomes the first man in space. His flight orbits Earth once and lasts for 108 minutes.

May and July: U.S. launches Alan Shepard and Virgil Grissom on 15-minute suborbital flights in Mercury capsules.

August 6: Cosmonaut Gherman Titov in *Vostok 2* makes the second orbital flight, spending more than a day in space.

1962

February 20: John Glenn becomes the first American to orbit Earth.

August 27: U.S. launches first successful planetary probe, *Mariner 2*, to Venus.

November: Construction begins on the Vehicle Assembly Building (VAB), on Merritt Island, adjacent to Cape Canaveral, Florida; serves as assembly area for the enormous Saturn V Apollo Moon rockets.

astronautics
The science of space travel.

ballistic missile
A rocket-launched missile whose flight arcs over and falls to Earth unpowered.

capsule
The name given to early manned spacecraft.

geostationary orbit
A space path of a certain speed and distance that keeps a satellite in the same location above Earth.

G-forces
The forces astronauts experience when their launching rocket accelerates quickly beneath them. These forces are several times greater than G, the normal pull of Earth's gravity.

gravity
The one-way force caused by the attraction of a large mass and the spin of that large mass, which exerts a "pull" on all other matter in the universe.

heat shield
A coating on the outside of a spacecraft that protects it from the extremely high temperatures generated during reentry into the atmosphere.

ICBM
Intercontinental ballistic missile; a long-range missile capable of travel from one continent to another.

IRBM
Intermediate range ballistic missile; a missile with a range of several hundred miles.

launch vehicle
A combination of rockets designed to lift objects into space.

meteorologist
A scientist who studies Earth's weather.

NASA
National Aeronautics and Space Administration.

orbit
The path of a spacecraft circling another body, such as the Earth or Moon.

payload
The cargo carried by a rocket or a launch vehicle.

probe
A spacecraft launched from Earth to explore distant bodies in the Solar System, such as planets, asteroids, and comets.

propellant
The fuel burned in a rocket to produce the hot gases that propel the rocket.

retrorocket
A rocket used to slow down a spacecraft. A spacecraft fires its retrorockets as a brake to reduce its speed so that it can fall down from orb

rocket
A self-contained engine that burns fuel in oxyge to produce a stream of hot gases. As the gases shoot out backward through a nozzle, the reacti propels the rocket forward. Because rockets carr their own oxygen supply, they work in space.

satellite
A smaller body that orbits around a larger one i space. Most of the planets have natural satellites or moons. Earth also has thousands of artificial satellites—spacecraft that humans launched into orbit around our planet.

solar cell
A device that harnesses the energy in sunlight a turns it into electricity.

sputnik
The Russian name for a satellite ("fellow traveler

stage
A rocket unit in a launch vehicle/step rocket.

step rocket
A rocket launch vehicle consisting of a number c rocket units, or stages, joined together. Each unit fires to burn its fuel and falls away when empty.

suborbital flight
A flight into space in which a spacecraft does no go into orbit.

weightlessness
The strange state astronauts experience in orbit, when their bodies—and everything else—appear to have no weight at all. The state is also called zero-G (no gravity).

BOOKS

Bilstein, Roger E. **Stages to Saturn: A Technological History of the Apollo/Saturn Launch Vehicles**. University Press of Florida, 2003.

Burnham, Robert. **The Reader's Digest Children's Atlas of the Universe**. Reader's Digest, 2002.

Cullen, David. **The First Man in Space: Days That Changed the World** (series). WAL, 2004.

Dickson, Paul. **Sputnik: The Shock of the Century**. Walker & Company, 2001.

Donkin, Andrew. **Space Stories that Really Happened**. Scholastic, 1999.

Exploring the Universe. 21st Century Science (series). World Almanac Library, 2001.

Furniss, Tim. **An Atlas of Space Exploration.** Gareth Stevens, 2000.

Miller, Jay. **The X-planes: X-1 to X-29**. Specialty Press, 2001.

PLACES TO VISIT

International Women's Air and Space Museum (Cleveland, Ohio) www.iwasm.org/

Intrepid Sea-Air-Space Museum (New York City) www.intrepidmuseum.org/

Johnson Space Center (Houston, Texas) www.jsc.nasa.gov/

Kennedy Space Center (Cape Canaveral, Florida) www.ksc.nasa.gov/

Neil Armstrong Air and Space Museum (Wapakoneta, Ohio) www.ohiohistory.org/places/armstron/

Pima Air and Space Museum (Tucson, Arizona) www.pimaair.org/

San Diego Aerospace Museum (San Diego, California) www.aerospacemuseum.org/

The Smithsonian National Air and Space Museum (NASM) (Washington, D.C.) Visit the largest collection of historic air and spacecraft in the world and touch a sample of lunar rock. www.nasm.edu/

Virginia Air and Space Center (Hampton, Virginia) www.vasc.org/

VIDEOS AND DVDs

A variety of space videos and DVDs are on sale at NASA visitors' centers and air and space museums.

Apollo 8: Leaving the Cradle Documentary with archive footage. Spacecraft Films, 2003.

Apollo 11: Men on the Moon Documentary with archive footage. Spacecraft Films, 2003.

Apollo 13 Movie starring Tom Hanks as Jim Lovell. Universal Studios, 2000.

The Mighty Saturns Documentary with archive footage. Spacecraft Films, 2003.

SPACE CAMPS

Florida, Alabama, and other locations host a number of space camps in the summer months. Lessons include learning about the nature and problems of spaceflight as well as hands-on experience in spaceflight simulators. **www.spacecamp.com www.vaspaceflightacademy.org**

WEB SITES

Animals in space—Learn about animal astronauts. www.stanford.edu/group/itss-ccs/project/spacedog /spacedog.gallery/laika http://ham.spa.umn.edu/kris/animals.html

GRIN: GReat Images in NASA—View one thousand historic photographs from NASA's collection. http://grin.hq.nasa.gov/

Imagine the Universe—Submit space questions here. http://imagine.gsfc.nasa.gov/docs/ask_astro/answers /970630a.html

NASA History—NASA's history office includes original documents, sound clips, and footage. http://history.nasa.gov/

NASA Kids—Information, games, and activities. http://kids.msfc.nasa.gov/

Space.com—The latest news about space exploration. www.space.com

Space Kids—Facts, information, and activities for tomorrow's astronauts. www.spacekids.com

Space Place—Things to make and do and interesting space facts. http://spaceplace.jpl.nasa.gov/

Yahooligans!—A selection of good space sites for kids. www.yahooligans.com/Science_and_Nature /Astronomy_and_Space/

INDEX

ABOUT THE AUTHOR
Robin Kerrod writes on space
and astronomy for a wide audience.
He chronicles the exciting events of
the space frontier in the following
best-selling titles: *Hubble, Apollo,
Voyager,* and the *Illustrated History of
NASA*. Robin is a former winner of
Britain's COPUS science book prize.